NEW

This edition published by
Barnes & Noble, Inc.
by arrangement with Brompton Books
Corporation

Produced by Brompton Books Corporation
15 Sherwood Place
Greenwich, CT 06830 USA

ISBN 0-7607-0412-0

Printed in China

Dearest Gail & Edward,
this is just a small remainder of
where the friendship started. It must
be fate that it continues 3,000
miles away.
                    Sincerely, Kreusje + Dejan
San Francisco, May 1987

YORK

TEXT	BARBARA PAULDING THRASHER
DESIGN	DON LONGABUCCO

BARNES & NOBLE BOOKS
NEW YORK

The author and publisher would like to thank the following people who have helped in the preparation of this book: Susan Bernstein, who edited it, and Rita Longabucco, who did the picture research.

1 One of New York City's most distinctive land-marks, the Empire State Building.

3-6 A sunset view of the southern tip of Manhattan, with the Statue of Liberty casting her own glow.

INTRODUCTION

New York is many things to many people. To the millions of people who live, work, or visit here, New York City has millions of different definitions. Yet on one point most people would have to agree: an extraordinary depth of diversity distinguishes the city of New York, setting it apart from the other large cities of the United States. Diversity in ethnicities and neighborhoods, architecture and activities manifests itself in a myriad of images—each image different but capturing a facet of the city. A woman feeding pigeons in Central Park, a couple on a bench sharing the newspaper, a street mime entertaining pedestrians, the gleaming towers of the World Trade Center, the intricately cabled Brooklyn Bridge, an elegant table in a posh restaurant, jubilant spectators cheering the Thanksgiving Day Parade, the spire of the Empire State Building disappearing in the clouds, the frenetic energy of a busy day in the Stock Exchange, the unexpected beauty of flowering trees in Battery Park, the magic of city lights twinkling at night—in each of these images a piece of the city can be discovered.

New York City is a business and commerce center; it's where the action is. Proximity to thousands of business headquarters and a multitude of networking opportunities have centralized many businesses here, including the glamorous fields of finance, publishing, advertising, jewelry, and fashion. Many people come to the city to seek their fortunes and fulfill their dreams in these, and other fields, and find themselves under the magical spell of New York's dynamic lifestyle, contemporary spirit, and cultural wealth. They become New Yorkers, addicted to the glitz, the vibrant street life, the feeling that something is always happening, the savvy that seems to border on smugness. Then there are the older New Yorkers, the people who have been born and brought up here—some representing the fourth or fifth generation of city dwellers. These people know an older, more mellow city, one that existed before the hyper-expansion of the past three decades. Vestiges of this city of the past still exist today, and all New Yorkers experience it, whether they know it or not. For in the midst of the ultra modernity of today's Big Apple are hundreds of small neighborhood niches. In these neighborhood havens people still linger on stoops swapping stories, children play stickball or hopscotch on the sidewalk, and colorful swatches of laundry connect apartment buildings. People do not drive their cars to malls to do their shopping; they walk, mesh bag or wheeled cart in hand, to local stores, where the same familiar faces greet them. Many of these neighborhoods represent ethnicities—most notably Chinatown and Little Italy—that feature their own traditional and colorful festivals. It is this old-fashioned face in the midst of the cosmopolitan city that lends depth and character to New York, making it a place that cannot easily be explained or dismissed.

The juxtaposition of old and new is also apparent in the city's architecture. Brownstone buildings, brick tenements, and gothic cathedrals exist side-by-side with angled skyscrapers of steel and glass. Newspaper and food vendors hawk their wares on the streets much as they did a century ago, but they may seem out of place before a chic window display of futuristic fashions or a glittering plaza featuring a stark form of modern sculpture. Even the people represent this intermingling of the past, present, and future, as any people-watcher perched on the steps of St. Patrick's Cathedral, or in an outdoor cafe in Greenwich Village, can vouch. Traditionally suited businessmen, smartly clad office workers, and new wave artists share the sidewalks with old-time shopkeepers and tradesmen. And if the urbanites may seem inured to both the wonder and the squalor of the city, it is because they take it in stride. They've learned to be directed in a place that pulls one in so many directions at once.

The form that New York City takes today, with busy Manhattan as the hub, surrounded by the other four boroughs, reflects the history of the city. Indians lived in the area long before the arrival of white man in 1624, when a Dutch expedition left settlers on Manhattan. On May 6, 1626, Peter Minuit bought Manhattan for the Dutch from the Man-a-hat-a Indians for trinkets valued at $24, and later named the settlement New Amsterdam. Almost 40 years later, during the second Anglo-Dutch War, British troops seized New Amsterdam from the Dutch, who yielded it peacefully. Charles II granted the settlement to his brother, the Duke of York, who renamed it New York. Although the Dutch recaptured the colony in 1673, they ceded it to Britain the following year. A century later, with a population of 25,000 and the New World's largest port, New York felt the effects of the Revolutionary War. The city was plundered and partly destroyed by fire, but by 1820 its population of 150,000 ranked it as the largest city in the country, and soon afterward the Erie Canal opened a new shipping route between East and West, making the city that much more viable. European immigrants, seeking a better way of life, began arriving by the thousands by mid-century, swelling the population further. By the turn of the century New York was the second largest city in the world, and many of the city's most distinctive and valued assets—Central Park, Carnegie Hall, the Brooklyn Bridge, and the Statue of Liberty among them—had already been created. New York moved forward with its own momentum, growing only larger and stronger despite the Great Depression—in the midst of which were erected the Empire State Building and Rockefeller Center—and the city's fiscal crisis of 1975. During the eighties a plethora of new luxury hotels and large skyscrapers were built, including the Trump Tower, IBM Tower, AT&T World Headquarters, and Jacob K. Javits Convention Center, giving New York an appearance of prosperity, despite the growing number of homeless people on the city streets.

New York is a city of ironies, glimpsed daily in such visions as that of a poor vagrant huddled near the resplendent Rockefeller Center. Of the city, Simone de Beauvoir wrote, "I shall never encompass New York in words. I no longer seek to encompass the city: I become dissolved in it. Words, pictures, knowledge, expectations are of no service: it is pointless to establish whether they are true or false. There is no confrontation possible with things to be encountered in New York. They exist in a fashion all their own: they are *there*. And I gaze and gaze, astonished as a blind man must be who has recovered his sight." New York *is* astonishing, not only in its sheer volume, intensity, and size, but by the fact that it was created by mere mortals. To stand atop one of the world's highest buildings and see cars cutting their way down an avenue lined with skyscrapers, like water coursing through the Grand Canyon, is to experience the heartbeat of New York.

Not all of Manhattan is laid out, however, in the convenient grid pattern that structures most of the island. From Greenwich Village to Battery Park there is a random arrangement of streets that reflects this area's past as a residential area for many of the city's workers. In 1811 the Commissioners Plan of New York imposed a gridiron street system on Manhattan from Houston Street to what would later become 155th Street. New York's many moods and aspects—from the glittering, fast-paced midtown; to the magical appeal of Broadway; to the enormous and stately Rockefeller Center; to the West Side, hub of America's classical performing arts with its Lincoln Center, which includes the Metropolitan Opera House, Avery Fisher Hall, Alice Tully Hall, New York State Theater, and the Juilliard School, and other great institutions; to the chic residential Upper East Side—are contained within Manhattan's 22 square miles.

Manhattan is the smallest of the five boroughs that make up Greater New York. Queens and Brooklyn, located on the western end of Long Island, Staten Island and the Bronx give the city a total land mass of 320 square miles, and a population of over seven million. More than two-thirds of the state's population live in New York City, which is serviced by 704 miles of subway tracks, and some 12,000 taxis. But the city is more than the sum of its parts. It is a legacy of the many great New Yorkers who have lived here, including John Jacob Astor, J.P. Morgan, Theodore Roosevelt, George Gershwin, Edward Hopper, Eugene O'Neill, and Walt Whitman. As large and complex as New York seems, it is a microcosm of something even greater. As H.G. Wells wrote, "To tell the story of New York would be to write a social history of the world."

THE BIG APPLE

The term "The Big Apple" conjures up images of all that is quintessentially New York—busy streets teeming with pedestrians and yellow taxi cabs, world famous buildings and statues, tourists and New Yorkers alike strolling through the Central Park Zoo, power-lunching executives in landmark restaurants, Mets fans doing the "Curly Shuffle" at Shea Stadium during the seventh-inning stretch, the awe-inspiring view of the lower Manhattan skyline as seen from the Statue of Liberty's crown. Yet New York City is much more than those things that are sought out by its 20 million visitors daily.

When the lighted big apple makes its annual descent into Times Square each New Year's Eve to mark for America the closing of one year and the beginning of the next, the city embodies the disappointments and hopes of a nation. While the exciting spirit of New York City, with its many attractions and activities, captivates visitors, New York's inhabitants have learned to accept and even enjoy, in a perverse way, the down side of the Big Apple. Though many would not admit it, they take a certain pride in knowing the ropes, using street smarts to get around by snagging the elusive taxi or negotiating the subway under-world, and in knowing where not to be and when not to be there. And, of course, they take a certain pride—but a pride that is never complacent—in living in the hub.

The Big Apple is the cultural center of the United States. With its unsurpassed number of theaters and museums, its concert halls, orchestras, dance companies, libraries, and its more than 50 universities and colleges, New York City has more to offer than a person has time to experience. The pulse of the city quickens after dark, as New Yorkers by the thousands turn out to dine and dance the night away. There is a restaurant and nightclub for every personality and mood, from chic to country, and from traditional ethnic to avant-garde.

The city also predominates economically, as a major financial center of the nation. Six of the country's seven largest banks are based in New York City, along with three of the five largest life insurance companies, a third of the largest retail firms, and almost 20 percent of wholesalers. While traditionally the industries of textiles, graphic trades, and foodstuffs have been the city's strongest, many other types of business headquarters have congregated here as well. The diversity and vitality of the Big Apple's business world lends vigor to the city by day, just as the exuberant entertainment world enlivens the city by night. Although New York City reflects and influences the trends and moods of the country, the Big Apple belongs to those who work and live here.

15 A seal suns himself in Central Park Zoo, where boulders juxtapose against skyscrapers.

16-17 Cruise ships dock on Manhattan's West Side, ready to carry New Yorkers from the city to the beaches of the Caribbean.

18 Tall ships moored at South Street Seaport speak of Manhattan's origins as a port city and major center for shipping.

19 Crates of fresh fish jam Fulton Fish Market in the early morning, as a busy day of buying and selling begins.

24 A dragon dance is performed in Chinatown during colorful Chinese New Year celebrations.

20-22 The southern tip of Manhattan, as seen from the Staten Island Ferry.

23 A statue of Prometheus presides over Rockefeller Plaza in midtown's Rockefeller Center. Located between Fifth and Sixth avenues, Rockefeller Center is a symbol of the power and wealth of New York.

25 Fans pack Shea Stadium in Flushing, Queens, to cheer their beloved New York Mets. With its many athletic teams, New York is a mecca for sports enthusiasts.

26-27 A sunny summer afternoon brings sunbathers to the green of Central Park, a haven for the busy urbanites. Central Park provides a range of recreational opportunities, including playing softball, jogging, bicycling, rowing, attending live performances, and strolling through the zoo.

28 The simple elegance of a table in the Russian Tea Room holds great appeal. Located on 57th Street near Carnegie Hall, this restaurant has long been a gathering place for performing artists.

29 The distinctive facade of New York's Hard Rock Cafe—one of the city's liveliest night-clubs—is unmistakable.

30 The World War II aircraft carrier, the Intrepid, harbors a fascinating sea, air and space museum.

31 Readers and pigeons loiter outside New York's impressive Jacob Javits Convention Center.

32 Workers on their lunch break lounge on the steps of St. Patrick's Cathedral, and watch the passers-by. People-watching is one of New York City's most popular pastimes.

33 The magnificent and serene interior of St. Patrick's Cathedral offers respite from the city commotion. Built between 1858 and 1878, St. Patrick's is the cathedral of the Roman Catholic Archdiocese of New York.

34 A hansom cab negotiates traffic near Central Park.

35 Visitors mill about in the elegant lobby of the Metropolitan Museum of Art. The Metropolitan houses one of the world's greatest art collections.

36 Snoopy and Woodstock are familiar and well-loved participants in the annual Macy's Thanksgiving Day Parade.

37 An elaborate float featuring Santa Claus and his reindeer is accompanied by lively Christmas trees, to end Macy's Thanksgiving Day Parade.

38 and 39 The landmark visage of New York's Statue of Liberty presides over the harbor. Designed by Frédéric Auguste Bartholdi, the statue was given to the United States by France in 1886 to commemorate their alliance during the American Revolution.

CITYSCAPES

Perhaps New York City's most recognizable and well-loved skyline, that of lower Manhattan as seen from the Brooklyn Promenade, seems as though it should have its own soundtrack. Etched by the silhouetted cables of the Brooklyn Bridge by night, the skyscrapers twinkling across the East River is a sight to soften the heart of even the most ardent Big Apple basher.

The many striking skylines and cityscapes of New York City are products of the curious melding of architectural styles representing different eras, and the wealth that procured expensive building materials and architects of distinction. The fact that four out of five of the city's boroughs are on islands (with the Bronx being the exception), affords a multiplicity of views across water. Although by the middle of the nineteenth century New York City's population numbered one million, buildings rarely exceeded five stories in height. The development of the elevator by the century's end facilitated the creation of taller buildings, and Manhattan soon began taking on a new shape as a skyscraper style emerged. Two of the earliest skyscrapers, the 31-story Park Row Building (1899) and the Flatiron Building (1902), demonstrate the compositional principles the city's early architects employed. The Empire State Building and Chrysler Building typify the next phase of building construction, as building regulations required that successive stages of a skyscraper be stepped back. Later, a popular trend emerged that allowed for areas of open space around the base of the building. This contemporary style can be seen in the fountains and atriums from which many of the city's modern skyscrapers can be viewed.

From many angles and sites, the World Trade Center dominates New York's skyline. The two 110-story towers of the World Trade Center, at 1,350 feet, is the city's tallest skyscraper. Although its twin towers have been criticized as lacking imaginative design, the brilliance with which the enormous reflective towers dazzle seems fitting for a city as bold and brash as New York. Then there is the Empire State Building—a sandstone and granite obelisk rising 1,250 feet into the sky—which can seem almost surreal to the first-time visitor, whose impression of the skyscraper may derive from King Kong movies. The Empire State Building is unquestionably the city's principle landmark, rivalled in the hearts of New Yorkers only by that masterpiece of art deco design, the Chrysler Building. With the characteristic pointed spire with arches and triangular, stainless steel windows, the Chrysler Building, like many of the city's inhabitants, has a style all its own.

Each of the city's skyscrapers has its own story, each one is a city unto itself—and together they make up the many cityscapes of the Big Apple. Viewed from across the East River, or from the top of the Empire State Building, or from the sanctuary of Central Park, New York's cityscapes derive their magical appeal from the diversity and enterprising spirit they represent.

41 The watery reflection of one skyscraper by another presents an abstract and appealing image.

42-43 A tall ship proceeding before New York City's distinctive downtown skyline presents a spectacular sight.

44 The art deco spire of New York's Chrysler Building reflects sunset light. Across the East River sprawls the borough of Queens.

45 Like the streets and avenues of Manhattan, a building reflection is segmented into a grid pattern. The juxtaposition of old and new is an appealing aspect of New York's architecture.

46-47 An early morning view across the water of Manhattan's southern tip. The Brooklyn and Manhattan bridges can be seen at right.

48-49 The twin towers of the World Trade Center dominate New York's financial district in this view of the southern Manhattan skyline across the East River from Brooklyn.

50 A wide-angle view of midtown Manhattan.
looking south.

51 A tugboat cruises past Liberty Island, where
Lady Liberty holds her beacon aloft.

52 Park Avenue at 50th Street, with the elegant
Waldorf-Astoria Hotel on the south corner and St.
Bartholomew's Church on the north.

53 The Lipstick Building (right) on Third Avenue
between 53rd and 54th streets, built in 1986, is
dwarfed by the landmark Citicorp Center.

54 (top) A wintry view of Central Park, as seen from midtown, with the George Washington Bridge (left) spanning the Hudson River.

54 (bottom) From the railroad yards on the West Side, corrugated boxcars create an interesting contrast to the skyscrapers.

55 Built between 1869 and 1883, the Brooklyn Bridge is regarded as one of the finest and most attractive examples of the marriage of technology and aesthetics.

56 Much of old New York has been razed to make way for the new, but enough of the early architecture remains to give depth and variety to the city neighborhoods. Here old and new coexist side by side.

57 A dizzying view of the World Trade Towers, stretching their lofty way 1,350 feet into the sky. Besides providing one of the city's most unmistakable landmarks, the World Trade Center houses offices for about 50,000 who work there.

58-59 The Brooklyn and Manhattan bridges stretch across the East River, from the southern tip of Manhattan to Brooklyn.

60-61 An aerial view of midtown with the Empire State Building dominating the skyline.

62 On Fifth Avenue between 58th and 60th streets, Grand Army Plaza provides a place to sit, play, or stroll.

63 The distinctive, triangular Flatiron Building is located on 23rd Street at the confluence of Broadway with Fifth Avenue. Erected in 1902, it is one of the city's first buildings to be supported on a steel frame.

64 Lines of rooftops represent parallel streets in New York's pleasant Brooklyn Heights neighborhood.

65 Workers on a movable scaffolding are dwarfed by the building's facade as they take a break.

PEOPLE

The more than seven million people who live in New York City, and the millions more who visit daily to work, shop or sightsee, imbue the Big Apple with a bustling vitality that is as exciting as it can be annoying. While the inexorable tide of commuters marching up and down the city's avenues can seem faceless and intimidating, daily life in the city is filled with moments of surprising intimacy, exuberance, and pathos. Impromptu sidewalk performances, the spirited participation in the city's many parades, festivals, street fairs, and outdoor concerts, and people lunching, strolling or sunning in parks give dimension to the Big Apple.

New Yorkers and visitors alike throng to celebrate—with fireworks and rowdy camaraderie—New Year's Eve in Times Square, Chinese New Year, and the Fourth of July. Local flavor emerges as New York's many ethnic populations display their wares and offer their cuisines at such annual celebrations as the Ukrainian Festival in May, or Little Italy's Feast of San Gennaro in September. The city's ardent Irish Americans close down midtown Fifth Avenue every March 17 for the jubilant St. Patrick's Day Parade. The following month the avenue takes on a different mood as the Easter Parade wends it way, in all its distinctive finery, from 49th to 59th streets. New York City's most bizarre and eccentric parade proceeds through Greenwich Village every Halloween, as outrageous costumes reflecting current events or personal idiosyncracies amaze onlookers. And the crowning event of New York's parades—Macy's Thanksgiving Day Parade—sends giant balloons and fantastic floats down the city's West Side.

New York's many festivals reflect the ethnic diversity of the city's population, the bulk of which is descended from late nineteenth- and early twentieth-century immigrants. Although New York City's population numbered only 5,000 in 1700, near the century's end the figure was 33,000, and in the following 10 years the population doubled, surpassing that of Philadelphia and making New York the young nation's largest city. The immigration explosion during the last half of the nineteenth century—comprised mainly of Irish, Germans, Italians, and Jews, but including Poles, Ukrainians, Czechs, Hungarians, English and Scottish as well—swelled the city population further. Although the immigration slowed after 1924 when quotas were imposed, World War II brought a renewed flow of immigrants seeking refuge, the increasing mechanization of agriculture brought black workers from the southern states seeking employment and better pay, and the tremendous tide of Spanish-speaking immigrants from Puerto Rico, the Caribbean, and Latin America made Spanish the city's second language. Rather than mingling into an urban melting pot, many groups maintain a strong sense of ethnic identity by settling neighborhoods with their own churches, shops, and restaurants. From black Harlem to the Latin American Barrio, from Brooklyn's Hasidic Williamsburg to Queens' Greek community in Astoria, the Big Apple has been carved into a multiplicity of niches.

But ethnic identity is only one aspect of the people of New York City. Diverse as they may be, there are many elements that bind New Yorkers together. The people who live and work in New York's metropolis thrive in the hustle and bustle, yet they enjoy the privacy, paradoxical as it may seem, that the city affords. They can take it or leave it, but all the city has to offer is there for them.

67 Joggers and pedestrians make their way across the Brooklyn Bridge.

68-69 A colorful crowd of Macy's Thanksgiving Day Parade spectators spills onto the street, as a policewoman keeps a watchful eye.

70(left) A smiling street vendor sells candy-coated peanuts. Although some consider street vendors a nuisance, many appreciate the convenience, and local color, that they offer.

70(right) Flags flap in the wind during a colorful parade in Chinatown.

71 A performer entertains during one of the city's many festivals.

72-73 Office workers enjoy their lunchtime break sitting near a fountain in the sun on Sixth Avenue.

74 A young woman disguised as the Statue of Liberty presents a remarkable verisimilitude.

75 A New York City mime, painted silver, performs on the streets.

76 *A couple shares the* Daily News *on a park bench.*

77 Boys launch a model sailboat on the lake in Central Park.

78-79 A solitary figure makes his way through Central Park in autumn. Designed in the mid-nineteenth century by Frederick Law Olmstead and Calvert Vaux, the park was designated a National Historic Landmark in 1965.

80 A Chinese performer demonstrates karate in
Washington Square Park.

81 The streets of Manhattan are enlivened by
such characters as this performing clown, who
inspires pedestrians to smile.

82 The doorman at New York's posh Trump Tower stands at attention.

83(left) A little girl wanders about a waterfront park in lower Manhattan.

83(right) A man ponders over his chess move in Washington Square Park, where city-provided chess tables entice players of all ranks and ages.

LIGHTS

The magic of New York City exerts its greatest pull after dark, when colorful lights from skyscrapers, shops and the street create a glowing mosaic. New York comes alive at night with a seemingly infinite variety of things to do. From the polished, spectacular Broadway shows to unusual, experimental Off-Broadway offerings, from famous comedy clubs to exclusive dance clubs, the Big Apple outdoes itself after dark.

Beckoning like a siren, the glow of the Empire State Building's lighted top can be seen at night from miles around. Floodlights illuminate the skyscraper's upper 30 floors, changing color to suit the season, except during the spring and fall bird migrations, when the lights are turned off so as not to confuse the birds. An unmistakable pattern of lights decorates the Chrysler Building after dark as well, and the slanted glow from the top of the Citicorp Building provides another urban reference point. Whether glimpsed from within Manhattan, from an evening Circle Line Cruise, from New Jersey or from another borough, the city lights at night hint at all that is contained within.

Just as the city's skylines appear most dramatic after dark, the many moods of the city are captured most dramatically then as well. The festive appearance of trees etched in white lights around the Tavern on the Green means something quite different from the neon cacophony of Times Square. The sight of the pendulous cables of the George Washington or Verrazano bridges twinkling in giant, sweeping curves excites a different sense than that aroused by the rushing white and red glow of city traffic. The scenes of the city seem more evocative at night, when patrons linger over coffee in a 24-hour diner, people fidget in line before a theater revue, or ice skaters whirl in the colorful glow of the Christmas tree at Rockefeller Center. Although window-shopping must suffice after dark in midtown Manhattan, downtown in Greenwich Village and other irrepressible neighborhoods, hundreds of small shops remain busy well into the night doing their trade in everything from bizarre jewelry and exotic art to souvenirs and trinkets. Out-of-towners seeking a thrill mingle with urbanites who display their idiosyncracies in unconventional fashions.

While, seen from afar, the thousands of lights that illuminate New York at night delineate the immensity and grandeur of the city, they also hint at the millions of lives being played out after dark in a city that never sleeps.

85 A view of the Empire State Building, bathed in red, white, and blue lights for the Fourth of July, looking south toward the twin towers and Battery Park.

86-87 City lights twinkle at dusk, and etch the outlines of the Brooklyn, Manhattan, and Williamsburg bridges spanning the East River.

88-89 A nighttime view of Manhattan and her sister borough of Queens, which sprawls east across the East River.

90 Madison Square Garden—site of many fine sports and entertainment events—casts an appealing glow at night.

91 The brightly lit Christmas tree at Rockefeller Center is a cheering sight amidst the city hubbub. Ice skaters enjoy the view and their sport at the same time.

92 A parade of heavy rush-hour traffic etches its
lights in this time exposure of the Brooklyn
Bridge at twilight.

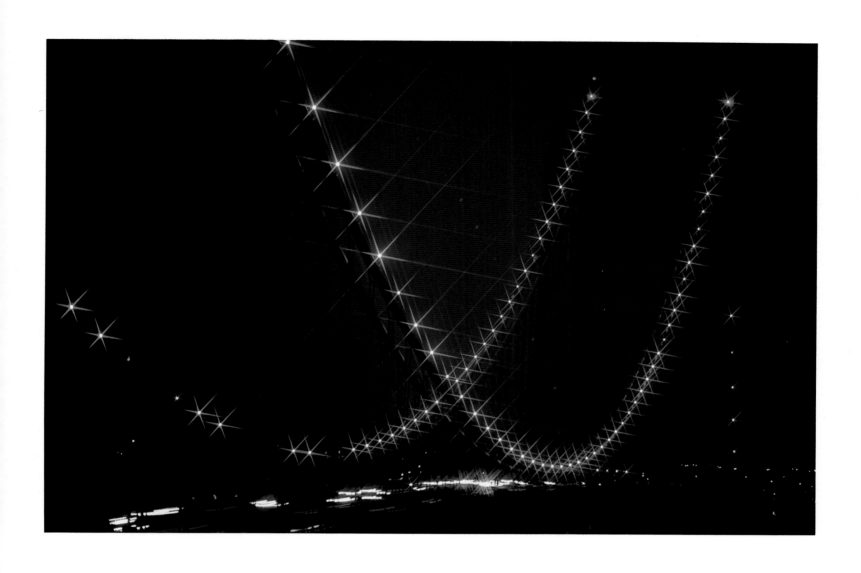

93 Viewed from Fort Lee, New Jersey, the enormous, looping cables of the George Washington Bridge twinkle at twilight. The bridge stretches 3,500 feet across the Hudson River.

94-95 The lights of Times Square turn night into day in the heart of Manhattan.

96 The magic of the city at night is apparent in this view of Manhattan, looking north from the World Trade Center. The towering spire of the Empire State Building, the sloping top of the Citicorp Building, and the art deco spire of the Chrysler Building are familiar sights.

97 The twin towers of the World Trade Center form the focal point of this nighttime view of lower Manhattan.

98-99 Cars and pedestrians bustle about midtown after dark—the city that never sleeps.

100-101 City lights reflect on the wet pavement at 72nd Street and Broadway; the IRT Control House was designed in a neo-Dutch Colonial style in 1904

102(top) Festively lit trees lend appeal to the Tavern on the Green near 67th Street and Central Park West. Located on the site of a late nineteenth-century sheepfold, the Tavern is an elegant restaurant.

102 (bottom) The spire of the Empire State Building appears to dissolve in the clouds in this eerie nighttime view.

103 Located between 33rd and 34th streets, the Empire State Building dominates this view down Fifth Avenue.

GLIMPSES

Can the city of New York be defined in her streets and avenues, skyscrapers and bridges, restaurants and theaters, people and events? There is the New York City that is evident while rushing to work, past familiar landmarks or strolling to a cafe rendezvous, but there are happenings and scenes in the city that defy classification and provide glimpses of something with a life all its own. These glimpses can be moments when an unexpected aspect of the city is suddenly perceived, when an irony, a detail, a hint of something greater, or an unusual juxtaposition gives immediacy to the city's identity. Although New York City can be described and explained in history and travel books, these glimpses—images with textures, sounds, and smells—evoke a tangible sense of place.

Features that make up the Big Apple, and endow it with a unique spirit, can be discovered in the spiraling ramp of the Guggenheim Museum, the stark outline of an ancient fire escape against a brightly painted wall, the blend of smells and small talk at a sidewalk hot dog stand, the people mesmerized by a juggler in Washington Square Park, the moment when the house lights dim at the Metropolitan Opera, the juxtaposition of flowers and concrete in Grand Army Plaza, the orange gleam of the twin towers at sunset, or the awe-inspiring sight of fireworks illuminating the Statue of Liberty. Moments in the Big Apple that capture a mood seem to transcend fashion and time, delineating a city that is at once impersonal and intimate, opulent and deprived, old and modern, futuristic and homespun. Glimpses into the core of the Big Apple can inspire a sense of camaraderie with the city that can suddenly imbue all those songs about New York with new meaning.

105 A girl jump-roping adds a touch of realism to this geometrically painted wall in one of the city's many pocket parks.

106-107 Concert-goers in Central Park enjoy the magic of listening to music in the open air and watching night come over the city.

108 Traders are busy at the New York Stock Exchange, where millions of shares are bought and sold each day.

109 A businessman takes a break to check up on the news.

110-111 An interior view of the Guggenheim Museum reveals the distinctive design devised by Frank Lloyd Wright, who supervised the Museum's construction in 1959.

112 A couple of New York pedestrians negotiate traffic downtown. The city's diversity allows its inhabitants to express their own styles.

113 A scofflaw feeds the pigeons in Central Park.

114-115 Bicycle parking is at a premium along this iron fence in central Manhattan. Despite heavy traffic, bicycling remains the transportation method of choice for many New Yorkers.

116 The interior of the Metropolitan Opera House; its grandeur complements the drama on stage.

117 A gleaming escalator curves upward from the lobby of the Trump Tower on Fifth Avenue.

118 French Gothic detailing on the window of an Upper East Side building provides a sample of the visual treats offered by the city's diverse architecture, if one only remembers to look up.

119 The stark geometry of a fire escape presents its own simple design.

120-121 A variety of international treats are available at this hot dog stand on the city street.

U.S.
GOV'T
INSPECTED

STICK
andwiches

122 A juggler entertains onlookers in front of Washington Arch on the north side of Washington Square Park. Before it was turned into a public park in the 1820s, the area that is now Washington Square Park was a burial place for the poor, and a site for hanging gallows.

123 Tulips and blossoming trees create a beautiful springtime scene in Battery Park.

124 The Plaza, built in 1907, is one of the few
buildings in New York City that can be viewed in
its entirety from two sides.

125 The majestic statue of General Sherman on horseback presides over Grand Army Plaza.

126 The twin towers of the World Trade Center are silhouetted against the sunset-colored sky.